Hildegard of Bingen

Hildegard of Bingen
Woman of Vision

To Karen —
May you be inspired!

Carol Reed-Jones

Paper Crane Press
Bellingham, Washington

Hildegard of Bingen: Woman of Vision

Cover and book design: Ellen Clark
Editing: Robin Ireland

Published by:
Paper Crane Press
P. O. Box 29292
Bellingham, WA 98228-1292
(360) 676-0266
To order retail copies, phone Book Clearing House at 1-800-431-1579.

Printed in the United States of America

Publisher's Cataloging-in-Publication
(Provided by Quality Books, Inc.)

Reed-Jones, Carol.
  Hildegard of Bingen : woman of vision / Carol
Reed-Jones.
    p. cm.
  Includes bibliographical references and index.
  SUMMARY: The life and works of Hildegard of
Bingen--nun, visionary, writer, composer, healer,
naturalist, traveling preacher, for young readers.
  Audience: Ages 10-14.
  ISBN-13 978-0-9650833-1-7
  ISBN-10 0-9650833-1-4

  1. Hildegard, Saint, 1098-1179--Juvenile literature.
2. Christian saints--Germany--Biography--Juvenile
literature. [1. Hildegard, Saint, 1098-1179.
2. Christian saints--Germany--Biography.] I. Title.

BX4700.H5R44 2004   282'.092
                    QBI04-700280

For creative people everywhere

Acknowledgements

Research for much of this book was made possible because of the existence of the International Society for Hildegard von Bingen Studies, which issues a newsletter twice a year covering the latest publications and research on Hildegard of Bingen. I am especially grateful to Dr. Werner Lauter, who graciously showed me some of his collection of books on Hildegard and took me on a guided tour of Hildegard sites.

I owe a great debt of gratitude to editor Robin Ireland, whose insight helped shape the manuscript into a stronger book. Book and map designer Ellen Clark created a wonderful cover that expresses the essence of Hildegard. My friends in three writing critique groups have patiently sustained me through many years of manuscript drafts. Medieval scholars Kari and Peter Diehl read the final draft and made comments. Marilyn McNaught gave excellent technical advice. Special thanks to Marrianne Heydron for her keen-eyed proofreading and layout suggestions.

Contents

Afterword

Preface

In 1995, when I was doing research for my Master's thesis in Music History, I was looking for an obscure woman composer to "discover." Hildegard of Bingen caught my attention immediately. Her music is unique. It is exciting, imaginative, innovative—and it is the largest amount of extant medieval music from any single composer.

So often in history, when a woman did something outside of the ordinary, she worked in obscurity, and her work might not be recognized or valued until well after her death. In contrast to this all-too-frequent scenario, Hildegard of Bingen was a woman who had been a composer nine hundred years ago *and* was well-known and admired during her lifetime. Hildegard was not obscure enough for my purposes, so I chose someone else for my thesis, but I thought, wow, what a life! She was so incredibly gifted and inspiring that I knew I had to write about her.

In Hildegard's life, as in the lives of many historical figures from hundreds of years ago, there are a few certainties, some gray areas, and a great many things that we may never discover. I have tried to stick to facts verifiable through translated primary source documents, or to theories by known Hildegard scholars. Any theories of my own are distinguished by qualifiers such as "might have," "may have," "could have," "perhaps," and similar wording. If something has been left out, either I did not feel that I could comfortably assert that it was true, or I did not have enough information to satisfy reader curiosity.

Some accounts of Hildegard and Jutta's enclosure in the anchoress' cell include a third girl with them, named Hiltrud. Her death date is just two years prior to Hildegard's. Some writers describe her as a nun in Hildegard's convent, her best friend, and a relative of Jutta's. Since this is the only information I have on Hiltrud, I decided that omission in this case was better than conjecture, and so she was not included in this biography. Future research may tell us more about her, but for now, there are more questions than answers about Hiltrud and her role in Hildegard's life.

Of the many books I consulted in my research on Hildegard and her times, two were particularly helpful. They are not listed in the bibliography, which is limited to books specifically about or by Hildegard, so I would like to acknowledge them here. For information about structures and ruins that Hildegard could have seen, I referred to *The Christian Travelers Guide to Germany,* by Irving Hexham and Lothar Henry Kope (Grand Rapids, Michigan: Zondervan, 2001). For information on ruins, and legends about some of the places Hildegard visited, the following rare book was very useful: *The Rhine From Its Source to the Sea* (2 vols.), by Karl Stieler, H. Wachenhusen, and F. W. Hacklander, translated into English by G. C. T. Bartley (Phildelphia: Henry T. Coates & Co., 1899).

Timeline of Hildegard's Life

1096   First Crusade.

1098   Hildegard is born.

1106   Hildegard goes to live with Jutta of Sponheim. She is eight years old.

1113   Hildegard becomes a nun at age fifteen, and is enclosed with Jutta as an anchoress at the Benedictine abbey at Disibodenberg.

1136   Jutta dies. Hildegard becomes the new *magistra* of nuns at Disibodenberg.

1141   Hildegard begins her first book, *Know the Ways*. At some time in the 1140s, she begins composing music.

1147   Second Crusade. The Pope reads parts of *Know the Ways* aloud at the Synod of Trier, a meeting of church officials. Church officials approve Hildegard's writings.

1150   Hildegard founds a new abbey at Rupertsberg near Bingen. She is fifty-two.

1151   Hildegard finishes *Know the Ways*. Richardis of Stade leaves Rupertsberg for a position as abbess in Bassum, 200 miles to the north.

1151-58   Hildegard writes *Natural Science*, *Causes and Cures*, and biographies of St. Rupert and St. Disibod.

1152   Richardis of Stade dies in Bassum.

1158   Hildegard begins *The Book of the Rewards of Life*.

1158-59	At age sixty, Hildegard begins her first preaching tour, to Mainz, Wertheim, Würzburg, Kitzingen, Ebrach, and Bamberg.
1160	Hildegard's second preaching tour, to Trier, Metz, and Krauftal. She preaches in public at Trier and Metz, an unusual privilege for a woman at the time.
1161-1163	Hildegard's third preaching tour. She visits Boppard, Andernach, Siegburg, Werden, and Cologne. She preaches in public in Cologne.
1163	Hildegard finishes *The Book of the Rewards of Life*, and begins *The Book of Divine Works*. On April 18, Emperor Frederick I (Barbarossa) issues an edict of protection for Rupertsberg.
1165	Hildegard founds a second abbey, Eibingen, at Rüdesheim.
1170	The fourth and final preaching tour. Hildegard, at age seventy-two, travels on foot or horseback to at least six monasteries: Eberbach, Maulbronn, Hirsau, Kircheim, Zwiefalten, and Hördt.
1173	Volmar, Hildegard's good friend and secretary, dies.
1174	Hildegard finishes *The Book of Divine Works*.
1178	An edict prohibits the singing of the Divine Office at Rupertsberg. The matter is resolved in March of 1179.
1179	Hildegard dies at age eighty-one on September 17, and is buried at Rupertsberg.

Map Legend

The places on the map are numbered in roughly the order they figured in Hildegard's history, except for her preaching tours. The places she stopped on her four tours are designated by symbols, a different one for the stops on each tour, rather than numbers.

1 Bermersheim: Hildegard's family home, where she was born.
2 Sponheim: Jutta's family home.
3 Disibodenberg: monastery where Hildegard and Jutta were enclosed. Their anchoress' cell later became a convent.
4 Clairvaux: Bernard of Clairvaux, later known as St. Bernard, was the abbot here.
5 Rupertsberg: the first convent Hildegard founded.
6 Stade: Richardis' family was from here.
7 Bremen: Richardis' brother Hartwig was archbishop here.
8 Bassum: Richardis left Rupertsberg to be an abbess here.
9 Eibingen: the second convent Hildegard founded.
10 Tholey: Hildegard's brother Roricus was a priest here.
11 Gembloux: Guibert, Hildegard's correspondent and later biographer, was a monk here.
12 Villers: The monks from here wrote, with Guibert of Gembloux, a long letter of questions to Hildegard.

Hildegard's Preaching Tours:

▲ Hildegard visited here during her first preaching tour from 1158 to 1159.

● Hildegard visited here during her second preaching tour in 1160.

▬ Hildegard visited here during her third preaching tour from 1161 to 1163.

♟ Hildegard visited here during her fourth preaching tour in 1170.

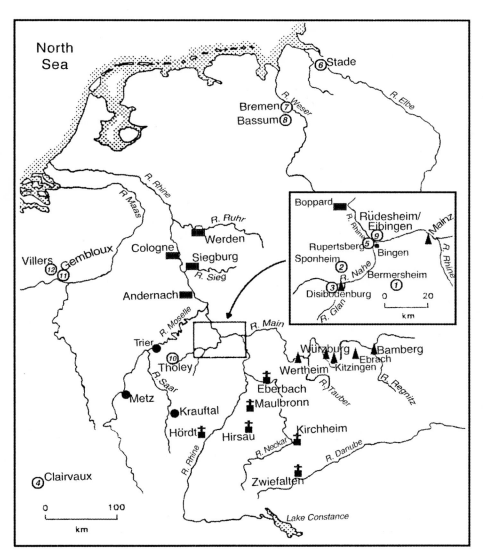

Map of Germany with places significant to Hildegard.

"I stretch out my hands to God
that I might be sustained by him,
just as a feather
lacking all force of its own strength
flies upon the wind."
Hildegard of Bingen in a letter to Guibert of Gembloux

Chapter One:
Child of Vision

"Look, Nurse!" Five-year-old Hildegard tugged on her nursemaid's hand. "What a pretty calf is in that cow over there—white with spots on its forehead and legs and back."

The nursemaid looked once, then looked again. A calf?! Where? There was no calf, just a large, pregnant cow. How could the child see an animal not yet born?

Amazed, the nursemaid told Hildegard's mother immediately. Hildegard's mother found out which cow it was, and asked to see the calf as soon as it was born.

The newborn calf looked exactly the way Hildegard had described it.

Hildegard of Bingen, youngest daughter of the knight Hildebert of Bermersheim and his wife Mechtilde of Merxheim, was born in 1098 in the village of Bermersheim, in what is now Germany. Besides her brothers Drutwin, Hugo and Roricus, and her sisters Irmengard, Odilia, Jutta, and Clementia, Hildegard had two other siblings whose names have been lost through the years.

Hildegard probably seemed like an ordinary child when she was born. The incident with the calf was strange enough that someone wrote it down, including Hildegard's words to her nurse. But that wasn't the first time Hildegard had seen something no one else could see. When she was three years old, she saw a light so bright that it frightened her. It frightened her even more to realize that no one else saw it. This ability to see things beyond the physical was an unusual gift, but because Hildegard was shy, these visions were sometimes a burden. She grew afraid of telling people what she experienced.

"I was quite exhausted by these things," she wrote years later, "and asked my nurse if she could see anything apart from outward objects. 'Nothing' she then replied, because she saw none of them. Then, seized by a great fear, I did not dare to tell about these things to anyone—although in my conversations and my lessons I used to announce many things about the future."

Hildegard found herself blurting out things that no one understood. She didn't want to, but almost against her will she would find herself commenting about what she saw. Sometimes she wept with embarrassment. And sometimes after a vision, she felt exhausted, even ill.

Regardless of how she may have felt about it, Hildegard's gift of sight would affect every part of her life, down to the smallest detail.

Chapter Two:
A New Beginning

What do you do when you have a daughter who: sees things no one else can; foretells events; is weak and has unexplained bouts of sickness; is timid, but blurts out the most unexpected things? Mechtilde and Hildebert must have asked themselves this at some point. Hildegard's gift of seeing probably convinced them that a life of prayer and contemplation was more suited to her than the other role most commonly available to young noblewomen of the time—that of wife and mother.

"In my eighth year," Hildegard wrote later, "I was offered to God for a spiritual way of life...." What did she mean by this? There are several schools of thought about it.

According to the traditional school of thought, in 1106 eight-year-old Hildegard joined fourteen-year-old Jutta of Sponheim, daughter of a family friend, in an anchoress' cell, where they expected to live for the rest of their days in isolation as religious hermits. Six years later, they took vows to become nuns. This interpretation of Hildegard's words has been accepted for several centuries.

Scholar Anna Silvas offers another way of thinking, based upon her research and translations of hard-to-obtain primary source documents. She thinks eight-year-old Hildegard and fourteen-year-old Jutta may have begun a regimen of study that lasted several years, reading scriptures, observing the hours of prayer with a pious woman named Uda, and living quietly at Jutta's home, and that this is the meaning of the autobiographical passage. Then, six years later in 1112, Hildegard and Jutta took vows to become nuns, undergoing the rites of anchoresses and entering the cell at the same time—or close to it. This seems more likely, since they would both have been of the age of consent then.

Jutta chose to be enclosed in a cell at Disibodenberg, a monastery closer to her home than to Hildegard's. St. Didibod, an Irish missionary, established the monastery over the site of an old Roman temple sometime around 640. Disibodenberg was built upon a hill between the Nahe and Glan rivers, and was under reconstruction from 976 until well after Jutta and Hildegard were enclosed in a cell there.

On the day they took rites, on November 1, 1112, the monastery church was filled with people, nobility and commoners, its interior ablaze with lighted tapers for the solemn induction ceremony. The bishop Otto had traveled over two hundred winding river miles from Bamberg to Disibodenberg to preside over the rites. It was unusual enough for a young woman to choose to become an anchoress, but here were two of them taking vows. Part of the ceremony included a funeral service to show that Jutta and Hildegard were no longer part of earthly life.

After repeating nuns' vows, fifteen-year-old Hildegard and twenty-year-old Jutta exited the church in a procession with the bishop, abbot, and monks, with the monks singing as they walked. The cell was only about twenty paces past the church door.

"This is my rest forever: here will I dwell, for I have desired it," Jutta and Hildegard sang from a psalm as they entered the cell. The bishop sprinkled dust over them as part of the funeral rites, while the monks sang another psalm.

"And so with psalms and spiritual canticles [they] were enclosed," Hildegard's twelfth-century biographer Guibert wrote. "After the assembly had withdrawn, they were left in the hand of the Lord. Except for a rather small window through which visitors could speak at certain hours and necessary provisions be passed across, all access was blocked off, not with wood but with stones solidly cemented in."

4

From excavations at Disibodenberg, archaeologists have found what they think may have been the cell in which Hildegard and Jutta were enclosed. Initially, it may have been smaller than the present-day ruins, which could include rooms added on later. The rectangular stone cell was about seventy-five feet long and faced the church entrance at an angle. It was divided into three small rooms, or two rooms and a garden plot, each about eighteen feet wide and less than fifteen feet deep. The cell probably had two windows, one to pass food and other items into and out of the cell, and one through which they could see and hear what went on in the church. Hildegard and Jutta may have slept on simple pallets and heated the cell with a metal brazier that held burning coals.

These are thought to be the excavated cell remains at Disibodenberg.

The clang of bells punctuated their days and nights. About every three hours, the bells rang, calling the entire monastery to one of the daily devotional services of the Divine Office. The devotional day began with Matins at midnight and Lauds at three—or Matins at two and Lauds immediately following, to give everyone more unbroken sleep before Matins. After Lauds everyone went back to sleep until

Prime at six in the morning. Tierce followed at nine; Sext at noon; None at three in the afternoon; Vespers at six; and Compline at nine. Then it was time for bed, until the bells for Matins woke them to start the cycle all over again. Hildegard and Jutta would have observed and participated in the devotions from their cell, using the window that faced into the church door. They would have been able to see and hear the services, and hear the chants sung at each.

In between the hours of the Divine Office, Hildegard and Jutta would have prayed, meditated, read scriptures such as the psalter (the book of psalms from the Old Testament of the Bible), and possibly done some sort of handwork considered suitable for young noblewomen, such as sewing and embroidering altar cloths and vestments. Hildegard may have learned to play the ten-stringed psaltery. It was plucked with the fingers, and could have been a tool for learning the music to the psalms, or music theory.

Their most frequent visitor was the young monk Volmar, who had been appointed to give them religious instruction and tutor them in Latin. He may have taught Hildegard simple psalm notation, so that she could record music pitches. Years later she would use it to write down the beautiful music she composed.

Chapter Three:
Convent Life

Years passed. Disibodenberg continued to grow, adding new buildings over the years. Hildegard probably saw and heard construction going on almost constantly: the scrape of mortar on stone, the clink of stonecutters carving, the clunk of heavy stone blocks dropping into place, the clang of glowing iron being pounded for hardware such as door hinges and grates like the one in the window of Hildegard and Jutta's cell. Since the monastery sat on the site of Roman ruins dating from the first through third centuries, artifacts several hundred years old could have come to light when workers laid building foundations or plowed garden plots.

In the region surrounding Disibodenberg, people talked about the two young women who had taken anchoress' vows at such an early age. Probably by word of mouth, Jutta became known as an anchoress and teacher, and Hildegard as her student. Parents of young noblewomen came to Jutta with requests. Could their daughters join her in a life of contemplation in the cell, and prepare to become nuns there? The families offered dowries of vineyards, properties and estates, which would provide income to pay for the support of their daughters at Disibodenberg.

Jutta referred the families and their offers of property to the abbot and senior monks. The abbot and monks encouraged her to accept the girls and teach them, and they added the girls' dowries of land to Disibodenberg's properties. The cell opened up and became a convent, with the women free to go outside. Jutta, however, chose to remain confined in the cell.

The convent grew, and Jutta was appointed *magistra,* or mistress, ultimately in charge of ten nuns. A *magistra* was like an abbess, but slightly lower in the church hierarchy. Disibodenberg became a double monastery, with monks in one wing, and nuns probably housed in the expanded cell.

Each day in a meeting called chapter, it was customary for the nuns to receive work assignments and discuss anything that affected the welfare of the convent. As *magistra*, Jutta would have matched each nun with work that used her talents or taught her something.

Some of the nuns may have worked in the monastery's *scriptorium*, copying manuscripts and creating documents with quill and ink on parchment from drafts made on wax tablets. Other nuns might have worked in the *herbarium*— the abbey's medicinal herb garden—made salves or potions, or cared for the sick in the *infirmarium*. They all probably shared the work of weaving fabric and embroidering ornate vestments and altar cloths.

Twenty-four years passed, years where no written record exists about either Hildegard or Jutta. Hildegard's talents and interest in music and healing hint to us that she might have been a chantress, leading the nuns in singing and teaching them new chants, and a worker in the *herbarium* and *infirmarium*. Otherwise, the rhythms of the convent— performing the Divine Office, contemplation, and daily work—likely filled her time as the seasons came and went.

At age thirty-eight, though, Hildegard's life changed forever.

Chapter Four:
New Responsibilities

After twenty-five years in the cell, Jutta died at age forty-five. She had been gradually getting weaker with each year, mostly due to her harsh ascetic discipline—constant fasting, wearing coarse hair garments that irritated her skin, standing for hours each day while she read the entire psalter through at least once.

The crowd for Jutta's funeral may possibly have been even larger than the one for her and Hildegard's induction ceremony twenty-four years earlier. Jutta had evidently been well loved. Men and women of all ages and stations in life attended, many weeping. According to the records of Disibodenberg, Abbot Kuno himself wept as he conducted the funeral.

Disibodenberg as it appeared around 1620-21.

With Jutta's death, the ten remaining nuns now needed a new *magistra*. They unanimously elected thirty-eight-year-old Hildegard, who declined, perhaps from modesty or from feelings of inadequacy. Abbot Kuno and the other nuns insisted, so Hildegard accept and became *magistra*, a teacher and leader of the other nuns.

Women and girls continued to join the convent, each bringing a dowry of money, lands, or other things that enriched the coffers of Disibodenberg. Rents on lands that Disibodenberg received helped them to support the growing community of monks and nuns, and this prosperity allowed them to offer the services of their *infirmarium* to the sick, and food and shelter to travelers. One of those to join the convent was Jutta's well-educated cousin, a young noblewoman named Richardis of Stade, who brought with her even more riches and prestige to the community.

During this time, Hildegard's visions, about which she had kept quiet for years, still continued. If anything, they were stronger than ever.

Chapter Five:
Visions of Light

One day, Hildegard stood trembling as her physical surroundings in the cloister washed away to insignificance in the blindingly bright light that came from...where? And the voice that spoke to her, where did it come from? It reverberated in her mind: "Frail human being, ashes of ashes, decay of decay, say and write what you see and hear! However, since you are timid in speech, simple in understanding and unlearned, the visions you write are not spoken and written from human interpretation, nor from human knowledge, nor brought forth by human will, but brought forth from the gift of heavenly sight: how you, in the wonder of God, see and hear."

Hildegard was forty-three years old, and sound of mind. She had experienced visions for most of her life, but from this vision, she understood she was to write them down. She hesitated. Who would believe her? Would people think she was presumptuous or only looking for attention? Would they think she was insane?

Greatly troubled, Hildegard took to her bed, literally sick with worry. She finally confided in Volmar, her former tutor, who was now the nun's chaplain. He was not as startled as he might have been, because Jutta had told him about Hildegard's visions years earlier. Hildegard wanted to know where these visions came from. She wrote to Bernard of Clairvaux, a monk already famous for his preaching, who would later be known as St. Bernard:

"I am very concerned about this vision which opens before me in spirit as a mystery. I have never seen it with the outer eyes of the flesh. And yet, already as a child, I saw great things of wonder which my tongue could never have given expression to, if God's spirit hadn't taught me to believe.

"I know in Latin text the meaning of the interpretation of the psalms, the gospels, and the other books which are shown to me through this vision. And yet this vision doesn't teach me writings in the German language; these I don't know. I can simply read them but have no ability to analyze them. Please answer me: what do you make of all of this?"

Bernard of Clairvaux replied:

"We rejoice in the grace of God which is in you. And, further, we most earnestly urge and beseech you to recognize this gift as grace and to respond eagerly to it with all humility and devotion, and with the knowledge that 'God resisteth the proud, and giveth grace to the humble.' But on the other hand, when the learning and the anointing (which reveals all things to you) are within, what advice could we possibly give?"

While Hildegard was probably grateful for Bernard's words of encouragement, she needed something more definite. Hoping for more tangible advice, she had Volmar speak on her behalf to their superior at Disibodenberg, Abbot Kuno. Abbot Kuno told Hildegard to go ahead and write down her visions. As she began to write, she recovered from her bout of illness.

Hildegard, Volmar, and Richardis of Stade worked out a system for recording her visions. First, she would write down what she had seen and heard on the wax tablets used for rough drafts. (The tablets were made of beeswax, melted and poured into a frame with a back that could be easily held and carried. Sometimes the frame hinged shut like a book.) Then Richardis would correct Hildegard's grammar. Finally, Volmar would copy it out neatly onto parchment.

Six or seven years went by, with Hildegard fulfilling her duties as *magistra* and writing down her visions when they came to her. Then, Pope Eugenius III found out about

Hildegard's visions and writings and sent two church officials to Hildegard to ask for a copy.

When the pope received a copy of Hildegard's writings, he read them aloud at the Synod of Trier, a major several-months-long church council meeting in late 1147 and early 1148. Bernard of Clairvaux attended and suggested that Hildegard be encouraged to continue writing. The pope gave his official approval. Hildegard was on her way to becoming famous.

Over the course of ten years, from 1141 to 1151, Hildegard wrote down twenty-six visions and compiled them into a book she called *Scivias*, or *Know the Ways of the Lord*. One of the original manuscript copies of this book, called the *Riesencodex*, is so large that it weighs about twenty-five pounds! It has beautiful, hand-painted illustrations, called illuminations, that some scholars believe were made by nuns under Hildegard's supervision. *Know the Ways* is the first of Hildegard's three major writings based on her visions.

"God gave you the best treasure, of course, your living intellect," Hildegard wrote in *Know the Ways*. "God loved you greatly because you are God's creature. And God instructed you with words about the established law, so that you might use your intellect to do good works and thereby profit. You are wealthy with virtues, so that God may be known as a loving and good giver because of this. Therefore it behooves you every hour to think about the ways you can make this grand gift which has been given to you useful to yourself and for others."

Hildegard was a firm believer in people using their talents. She spent most of her life finding and using her own gifts.

Chapter Six:
Composer, Poet, Linguist

Hildegard's creativity manifested itself in many ways. Music was one of them. It held such an important place in her life and thoughts that it often pops up as a metaphor in her writings. In a discussion about nature, she wrote, "When it turns, the firmament makes beautiful music which we, however, do not hear because of its great height and breadth."

Most women weren't taught music composition in the Middle Ages. It was part of the *quadrivium,* the four mathematical sciences—music, arithmetic, geometry, and astronomy—that young noblemen studied. Hildegard didn't let this stop her from writing music. Since 1112, when she and Jutta arrived at Disibodenberg, she had heard all 150 psalms sung each week as part of the Divine Office. Somehow, possibly through Volmar, she had learned simple psalm notation. Some scholars think she may have had access to writings about music theory. At any rate, she wrote her own words and composed exquisite music. She wrote some of her music at the request of other convents and monasteries, for occasions such as the dedication of a church or a special feast day. She gained recognition as a composer even before *Know the Ways* was completed:

"It is reported that, exalted, you see many things in the heavens and record them in your writing, and that you bring forth the melody of a new song, although you have studied nothing of such things," Odo, professor of theology at the school that would later become the University of Paris, wrote to Hildegard in her fiftieth year. "This does not surprise us at all," he continued.

Hildegard, who most likely would not have been allowed to attend the school as a woman, had received recognition from a faculty member at one of the most prestigious institutions of learning in the world.

The music Hildegard heard and sang was what we now call Gregorian chant. It had a free-flowing rhythm. The notes moved mostly by step, from one note to its nearest neighbor. When there was a leap, it was usually just a skip of one or two notes, and it was filled in immediately by stepwise notes. Much of Hildegard's music has wider leaps and is bolder and more exciting than other composers' music written in her time. Today, seventy-seven of her songs have survived the centuries, the largest amount of music to come down to us from a single medieval composer.

Below are the translated words, and on the facing page, the words with music, to Hildegard's song, *Laus Trinitati*. The words with music are arranged for a hymnal. Notice the wide leap at the beginning, between the first two notes. This type of leap is Hildegard's musical signature. Also, notice the difference in the translations on this and the facing page. The translation on this page gives a more exact meaning of the original Latin words. The translation on the facing page allows people to sing the song in another language.

Laus Trinitati

Praise to the Trinity,
which is sound and soul
and life-cause of all beings,
and which is the praise of the angelic host
and wonderful brightness of hidden secrets
of which humankind is unaware,
and which is the life in all.

Laus Trinitati
O praise be to you Holy Trinity

Laus _____ Tri - ni - ta - ti
O _____ praise be to you Ho - ly Tri - ni - ty

quae so - nus et vi - ta
re - soun-ding ju - bi - la - tion and life of all that is.

ac cre - a - trix óm - ni - um in vi - ta ip - so - rum est.
To our Moth-er Great Cre - a - tor of all things liv-ing and of life it - self.

Et quae Laus an - ge - li - cae tur - bae.
O an - gel - ic cho - rus soun-ding forth in joy - ful praise!

Et mi - rus splen - dor ar - ca - no - rum
O the won-der - ful si - lent splen - dor of the ho - ly mys - 'tries

quae ho - mi - ni - bus ig - no - ta sunt est
Tri - ni - ty shin-ing bril - liance un - known to wo - men or to men.

et quae in om - ni - bus vi -
O quick-en - ing spar - kle dwell-ing in all! Life - giv - ing Life!

- - - - ta est.
Life of all things glo - rious - ly cre - a - ted!

The slurs indicate the chant flow in groups of twos and threes.

Words: Hildegard of Bingen (1098-1179); tr. Lisa Neufeld Thomas © 2001 Lisa Neufeld Thomas. All right reserved. Used by permission.

Music: Hildegard of Bingen (1098-1179); tran. Lisa Neufeld Thomas © 2001 Lisa Neufeld Thomas. All rights reserved. Used by permission.

17

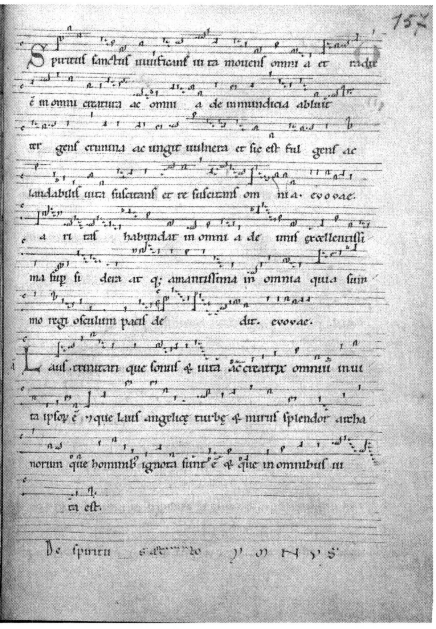

An original manuscript of Hildegard's music. The song Laus Trinitati *starts at the large letter L, a little more than halfway down the page. Facsimile copyright Alamire Music Publisher.*

Sometimes Hildegard's creativity took an interesting turn. She invented her own twenty-three-letter alphabet, *Litterae Ignota,* or *Unknown Letters.* She also invented a 900-word secret language, *Lingua Ignota,* or *Unknown Language.* In one of her songs, *O orzchis Ecclesia*, she used this secret language in a poetic way. She substituted five of her invented words in that song—the only time she used her invented language as poetry. *Unknown Language* is a fascinating mix of German, Latin, and other sounds. Many linguists, or language scholars, have been interested in it over the centuries, including Wilhelm Grimm, who was also one of the authors of *Grimm's Fairy Tales*!

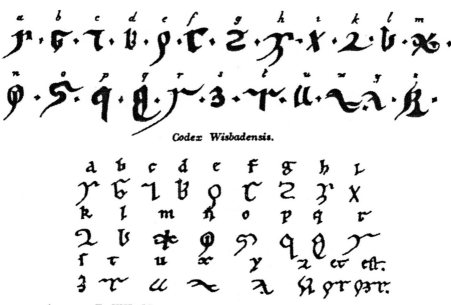

Codex Vindobonensis.

Codex Wisbadensis.

ANALECT T. VIII. 33

Hildegard's alphabet, as it appears in two different manuscripts.

Chapter Seven:
Diplomat and Correspondent

With all the attention that her writings and music brought, Hildegard became a celebrity. Rulers, both religious and secular, wrote to her for advice, and she replied. A collection of over 400 letters she both wrote and received has remained intact to this day. Hildegard didn't wait for people in power to write to her, though. If she felt something needed correcting, she wrote to the person responsible, in the same way we write to government leaders today to make them aware of situations we would like to change. Hildegard's correspondents included kings and queens, emperors and empresses, popes, bishops, and other religious leaders, abbots and abbesses—men and women from many different stations in life. Her letters weren't always tactful.

"I see you as both a baby and a madman," she told Emperor Fredrick I. "You neglect justice," she told Pope Anastasius IV. "Your heart is truly full of good will, so that you would gladly do good things, as long as the bad habits of mankind don't trip you and ensnare you for awhile. Be resolute and flee them!" she wrote to King Henry II of England. To his wife, Eleanor of Aquitaine, one of the most powerful women of all times, Hildegard was sympathetic and encouraging. "Stand unwavering before God and mankind. God will help you in all your sorrows."

Hildegard's correspondents were respectful—with one exception. Tengswich, the *magistra* of the St. Marien convent at nearby Andernach, wrote to Hildegard:

"The report of your saintliness has flown far and wide and has brought to our attention things wondrous and remarkable. And insignificant as we are, these reports have highly commended the loftiness of your outstanding and extraordinary mode of religious life to us. We have learned from a number of people that an angel from above reveals many secrets of heaven for you to record, difficult as they are for mortal minds to grasp, as well as some things that you are to do, not in accordance with human wisdom, but as God himself instructs them to be done."

Hildegard was probably not pleased with Tengswich's sarcastic, disdainful tone, but we know that she read the entire letter.

"We have, however, also heard about certain strange and irregular practices that you countenance," Tengswich continued—and she listed all the rumors she had heard.

Tengswich referred to the fact that unlike most nuns, who wore simple unadorned black habits year-round, Hildegard's nuns dressed entirely differently on religious feast days. Their hair was unbound, and they wore floor-length white silk veils, gold rings on their fingers, and gold filigree crowns with religious symbols on them—crosses on the sides and back, and a lamb on the front.

"Moreover," Tengswich's letter read, "that which seems no less strange to us is the fact that you admit into your community only those women from noble, well-established families, and absolutely reject others who are of lower birth and of less wealth. We have examined as accurately as possible all the precedents laid down by the fathers of the Church, to which all spiritual people must conform, and we have found nothing in them comparable to your actions."

"Therefore, we have decided to send this humble little letter to you, saintly lady, asking by whose authority you can defend such practices, and we devoutly and meekly beseech, worthy lady, that you not disdain to write back to us as soon as possible."

These were serious charges, possibly enough to get Hildegard in trouble with church authorities. She needed to answer Tengswich and her nuns, not meekly, but justifying her actions with calm authority.

Why did her nuns wear special clothes, jewelry, and gold crowns on feast days? Because they were brides of Christ, and dressed as brides on holy days.

The most serious charge was also the last. Why did Hildegard admit only high-born nuns in her convent? We can only guess. Perhaps Disibodenberg was not completely self-sufficient and needed the income from properties that wealthy noble families gave as dowries when their daughters joined the convent.

Some scholars think that Hildegard may have believed, as did most people of her day, in the concept of three ranks of society—nobility, religious, and peasant. Nobles could take religious vows, and potentially attain high positions within the church hierarchy. Peasants who wanted to join themselves to a religious community might become lay (secular) members, mostly performing manual labor.

Another possibility is that Hildegard may have believed that some lower-born women might join a particular convent, not for spiritual reasons, but as a means of bettering their social standing by associating with the higher nobility. Women of the upper nobility did not gain in worldly honor because of joining a convent, but those of lesser birth may have thought they would gain such honor. Part of Hildegard's answer to Tengswich may reflect her thoughts about this:

"Where humility is found, there Christ always prepares a banquet. Thus when individuals seek after empty honor rather than humility, because they believe that one is preferable to the other, it is necessary that they be assigned to their proper place."

Did Tengswich's letter make Hildegard rethink her position on who she accepted into her convent? We don't know. Still, many years later, Hildegard would have a place for some of the women who were now excluded.

Chapter Eight:
Rupertsberg, a New Home

As time passed, the small cell that had been turned into a makeshift convent wing became too small for the number of women it housed. In 1148, the same year the Synod of Trier ended, Hildegard envisioned a new place for her nuns—literally. In her vision she saw a hill overlooking the joining of the Rhine and Nahe rivers. This hill, called Rupertsberg, which means "Rupert's hill," stood forty miles north of Disibodenberg, near the ruined castle of the Dukes of Bingen. Rupert, one of the dukes, lay buried there, and had been canonized a saint—St. Rupert.

The vision gave Hildegard resolve. The crowded convent, and the fact that the monks had control of the dowries the women brought with them, may have convinced her it was time for her nuns to move from Disibodenberg to a place of their own. However, the Disibodenberg monks and other church officials were very opposed to the move and wanted Hildegard and her nuns to remain there, perhaps because Hildegard's fame had brought many visitors and much money to the abbey. Still, Hildegard persisted. She knew it was right for the nuns to have their own convent, separate from the monastery.

Fortunately, Hildegard had an influential friend, the Countess of Stade, the mother of Hildegard's writing assistant, Richardis of Stade. The countess spoke to Abbot Kuno's powerful superior, the Archbishop of Mainz, about the move. Her influence helped Hildegard—but the countess had other plans for her daughter.

Finally, in 1150, the Archbishop of Mainz gave Hildegard permission to found an abbey at Rupertsberg. She and twenty nuns moved from their established quarters at Disibodenberg to the few old, disused buildings remaining at Rupertsberg. A large group of relatives and other folk accompanied them. As they approached Bingen, they were met by crowds of people, noble and common, dancing and singing to welcome them!

The nuns most likely had servants and hired workers for the restoration and expansion of the existing buildings, but still, the task was overwhelming, despite the welcome they received from the townsfolk. Hildegard's high-born nuns didn't make things any easier. Some complained incessantly, others simply left. Hildegard wrote:

"I then took up residence at this place with twenty aristocratic nuns who came from rich parents. There we found no inhabitants except an old man, his wife, and children. Such a great unpleasantness, distress, and work-overload overcame me like a storm cloud covering the sun. People shook their heads at me and said: 'What use is it that noble and rich nuns are moved away from one place where they have everything to a place where there is need?' We however hoped that the grace of God who had shown us this place would be with us."

One of the nuns who left was Richardis, Hildegard's writing assistant who had become like a daughter to Hildegard. As part of the Benedictine Rule, nuns and monks were supposed to commit themselves to staying in a single establishment without moving from one to another. Contrary to this, Richardis' mother and her brother, Hartwig, the Archbishop of Bremen, had found another place for Richardis. She would be abbess of Bassum, near Bremen, far from the Rhine valley.

Hildegard was devastated by what she saw as Richardis' desertion. She wrote letters of protest all the way up the ecclesiastical chain of command, from abbot to archbishop, even to the pope. Her efforts were futile. Richardis departed for Bassum, leaving a desolate Hildegard behind. It was just one more difficulty in the move to Rupertsberg.

Fortunately, those people who had criticized Hildegard and the nuns for the move eventually began to help them, giving them donations of money and land that yielded income from the rents paid by tenant farmers. Also, noble families asked for permission to bury their relatives in the cemetery, for which they were willing to pay handsome sums of money. Rupertsberg began to grow, with the addition of a scriptorium and workrooms.

The sturdy convent church took shape. A little over ninety feet long and about fifty feet wide, it had two towers. One side wall had a view of the Nahe River. Nearby was the chapter house, where the nuns had their daily chapter meetings. Eventually, a stone wall surrounded the convent property, enclosing the nun's dormitory, a chapel and churchyard, housing for the prior, and the convent garden— which was large enough that two acres of it were planted as a vineyard.

Rupertsberg. Engraving after a drawing by Daniel Meissner before 1625.

Just three years after the move to Rupertsberg, Hildegard would have to challenge the abbot of Disibodenberg for the right to keep the properties her nuns brought as dowries when they joined the convent. The monks of Disibodenberg had a hard time letting go of those properties with their profitable crops and rents.

In the meantime, work at Rupertsberg continued. Everyone focused on preparations for the dedication service for the abbey church that would take place on the first of May, 1151.

For ten years, Hildegard had been working on *Know The Ways*—since 1141. She finally completed it in 1151. She wrote the book's final vision in the form of a play set to music, *Play of the Virtues*, or *Ordo Virtutum*, and taught it to her nuns to perform at the dedication service for Rupertsberg's church. *Play of the Virtues* has women's singing parts for seventeen virtues, such as Humility, Hope, Innocence, Mercy, Discretion, Faith, Obedience and Charity. "We virtues are in God and we remain in God; we are soldiers for the king of kings and we overcome evil by good," they sing. The only man's part is also the only spoken part: that of the devil. Hildegard probably intended for Volmar to play that part, undoubtedly a good joke on him. *Play of the Virtues* is quite possibly the first morality play ever written. It has been rediscovered in the twentieth and twenty-first centuries and is still performed today.

Just five months after the dedication service, Richardis, who missed Hildegard and her community of nuns, tearfully begged her brother for permission to return to Rupertsberg—but it was too late.

Chapter Nine:
Naturalist, Healer

"Hartwig, archbishop of Bremen, brother of the abbess Richardis...to Hildegard, mistress of the sisters of St. Rupert," the letter began.

Hildegard must have wondered why Hartwig would write to her, after she had opposed Richardis' move from Rupertsberg so strongly. Perhaps she had a flicker of apprehension before she read Hartwig's next words:

"I write to inform you that our sister—my sister in body, but yours in spirit—has gone the way of all flesh, little esteeming that honor I bestowed upon her."

Richardis, Hartwig's sister, who had been so like a daughter to Hildegard and such a support in the writing of *Know the Ways*, was gone, dead of a sudden illness. Hildegard read in Hartwig's letter that Richardis had even pleaded, on her deathbed, to be allowed to return to Rupertsberg. If only she had not left in the first place...

What could she say to Hartwig, after their conflict over Richardis' departure? Hildegard managed to be generous even in her grief:

"Now you, dear Hartwig...fulfill the desire of your sister's soul, as obedience demands. And just as she always had your interests at heart, so you now take thought for her soul, and do good works as she wished. Now, as for me, I cast out of my heart that grief you caused me in the matter of this my daughter."

As if to keep her mind from sorrow, Hildegard threw herself into her work and new writings. One undertaking was a catalog of the natural world and its properties, called *Natural Science*, with categories for plants, trees, animals, reptiles, fish and things that swim, birds and things that fly, elements, stones, and metals. In it, Hildegard describes more than 170 animals, and over 250 plants, including trees. She has invertebrates such as the earthworm and slug in her list of reptiles, her list of fish includes the sea lion, and she groups flying insects with birds. The scientific system we use for naming and classifying plants and animals today was developed by Linnaeus 600 years after Hildegard wrote *Natural Science*. Hildegard was one of the first women naturalists.

In some ways she was ahead of her time. "The best grain is spelt," Hildegard wrote in *Natural Science*. "Eating it rectifies the flesh and provides proper blood. It also creates a happy mind and puts joy in the human disposition. In whatever way it is eaten, whether in bread or in other foods, it is good and easy to digest." Interest in spelt has revived in recent years, and its many nutritional benefits have been researched and documented.

Hildegard worked on and finished *Natural Science* and another book of remedies and natural history, *Causes and Cures*, between 1151 and 1158. She even includes remedies for animals in *Causes and Cures*:

"If sheep become sick, take fennel and dill in such a mixture that there is more fennel than dill; place them in water so that the water takes on their taste, give this water to the sheep to drink, and they will improve."

In *Causes and Cures*, Hildegard also writes of humanity's place in nature.

"Just as everything casts its shadow, in the same way man is the shadow of God, and the shadow is the visible sign of his creation. Man is the clear pointer toward almighty God in all of his wonders. He himself is a shadow because he has a beginning; God, however, has neither beginning nor end. For that reason, the harmony of the heavens is a mirror of the divinity, and man reflects all the wonders of God."

Many scholars consider Hildegard to be the first German woman doctor. Today, there is a renewed interest in her work by a small number of doctors who use some of her healing methods.

Chapter Ten:
Journeys of Discovery

At age sixty, Hildegard's life took a new direction, even while she was in the middle of a painful illness. She wrote that she felt as if her body was being cooked in an oven. Still, she persisted in her newest endeavor.

"During the time that I was still suffering from this pain," she wrote, "I was warned in a true vision to go to the site [Disibodenberg] which had been revealed to me by God and to speak the words revealed to me by God. That I did, but I returned to my daughters [nuns] with the identical pain. I also traveled to the other cloisters and taught there with words that God had commanded me."

After Disibodenberg, Hildegard traveled along the twisting and winding Main River, the largest secondary branch of the Rhine, visiting towns and monasteries along the way and preaching to clergy. While women were not expressly prohibited from preaching, it was an unusual thing for a woman to do.

Hildegard's closest stop was Mainz, where the substantial Main River empties into the Rhine. She could have seen eleven-hundred-year-old Roman ruins: an aqueduct and the posts of a stone bridge that once crossed the Rhine. The vast, solemn cathedral, with its massive bronze doors and the tomb of Charlemagne's wife, was much newer—it was only 160 years old.

Wertheim, where the Main and Tauber rivers meet, was the next closest town, nestled between two forests. In Würzburg she could have seen the first stone bridge ever built over the Main River, joined pilgrims at the church of St. Kilian, the city's patron saint, or visited St. Mary's chapel, a round stone church built 450 years earlier. We know she stopped at the convent at Kitzingen and the monastery at

Ebrach. She traveled as far as Bamberg, imperial residence and thousand-year-old city. It was from here that Bishop Otto had journeyed forty-five years earlier to Disibodenberg to hear her and Jutta repeat their vows.

At Würzburg and Bamberg she preached to clergy and the public, probably in the cathedrals there. This shows the extent to which she was respected and honored. Her entire journey was about 400 miles round trip, by boat, horseback, perhaps even on foot, and lasted several months between 1158 and 1159. There was much for her to see: astonishing cathedral architecture and art, different kinds of fish and birds, and traces of Roman ruins, all fascinating to a thinker like Hildegard.

Hildegard started *The Book of the Rewards of Life,* her second major book of religious writings, the same year she began her preaching tour.

"Reason is like a trumpet with a living voice," she wrote. "It fulfills its responsibility when it dispenses itself by various methods into creatures and in so far as the various creatures assist it so that they return a good and strong sound. But man's soul also has harmony in itself and is like a symphony."

In 1160, the year after her return home, Hildegard set out on a shorter trip, this time down a different tributary of the Rhine. She journeyed to Trier and Metz on the Moselle River, preaching to both clergy and townspeople there, as she had at Würzburg and Bamberg on her previous tour. She traveled to Krauftal, a convent on the Saar River, a tributary of the Moselle.

Hazzecha, abbess of Krauftal, wrote to Hildegard for advice after her visit. Hazzecha felt inadequate in her role as abbess, and overwhelmed—actually terrified—by the burden of all her duties. Should she follow her inclination to escape the tremendous pressure of her office by becoming an anchoress with two other friends? Hildegard replied to her in a letter,

"My dearest daughter, I do not see that it is profitable for you and those two close friends of yours to seek out a hermitage in the forest, or even the shrines of saints, since you have been sealed with the seal of Christ, by which you make your way to the heavenly Jerusalem. For if you undertake greater toil than you can endure, you will fall...."

Hildegard often encouraged individuals to fulfill their responsibilities, even when they had difficulties. Here she seems to imply that if Hazzecha went ahead and became an anchoress, isolated in the forest with two other women, she would experience less peace and even more stress than with her present duties.

Besides practical advice, Hildegard's letter had encouragement and inspiration as well: "I will also pray that you will perfectly complete the labors of holy works with pious discernment that, strengthened by the splendor of unsullied holiness and enkindled by the ardor of God's true love, you will achieve the perfect bliss in which you will live forever."

Hildegard had scarcely returned home before she began a third preaching tour that took place between 1161 and 1163, this time along the Rhine, past castles and steeply-planted vineyards, where the river flows northwest toward the sea. She visited the convent of St. Marienberg in Boppard, and may have heard a romantic legend associated with its origin. A knight named Conrad of Bayer had been paying court to Mary, a noble maiden. It was rumored that they were betrothed. However, Conrad's feelings toward her changed, and he made plans to leave Boppard and Mary to join the crusades. The day he left town, Mary confronted him. Dressed in armor with a closed visor and a shield emblazoned with the family crest, she masqueraded as her brother recently returned from the Holy Land. She challenged Conrad to mortal combat to avenge the insult on her honor. He fatally wounded her, and when he removed her helmet to try to help her, he discovered he had killed his betrothed. In sorrow, he had the convent of St.

Marienberg built, joined the Knights Templars, and went on crusade, where he died in battle.

Downstream from Boppard, Hildegard visited the convent of St. Marien at Andernach, from where the *magistra* Tengswich had written her mocking letter to Hildegard. From there she went further downstream to Siegburg, where the River Sieg joins the Rhine.

The monastery Siegburg sat on a huge rock overlooking much of the valley below, its appearance giving no hint of its violent origins. Count Henry the Furious, also lord of the town of Siegburg, was both a madman and a murderer. During one of his sporadic fits of madness, he set fire to his own town and slaughtered any citizens in his way. He spent the rest of his life locked up under heavy guard, and a monastery was built at Siegburg as a way of purging the memory of his evil deeds from the land.

The next city downstream where we know she stopped was Cologne, the grandest on this tour, pilgrimage site of St. Ursula and city of ecclesiastical power. Here Hildegard spoke in the cathedral to both clergy and townfolk.

"'The one who was, and is, and is about to come' speaks to the shepherds of the church: I set you like the sun and the other luminaries so that you might bring light to people through the fire of doctrine, shining in good reputation and setting hearts ablaze with zeal."

The opening words of Hildegard's sermon seemed to honor the clergy, but she also had some harsh criticisms.

"You are worn out by seeking after your own transitory reputation in the world, so that, at one moment, you are knights, the next slaves, the next mere jesting minstrels, so that in the perfunctory performance of your duties you sometimes manage to brush off the flies in the summer."

So much for those earlier uplifting words of praise! If the clergy had hoped for a comforting sermon, they must have been dismayed with Hildegard's description of their faults.

"Through the teaching of the Scriptures, which were composed through the fire of the Holy Spirit, you ought to be the corners of the Church's strength, holding her up like the corners that sustain the boundaries of the earth."

Hildegard gave her listeners a final warning as well as some encouragement:

"In your times, however, you will be engaged in restless wars on account of your desires and your unsettled morals, and through them, you will be reduced to nothing. But let each, to the best of his ability, escape them through good works and the safe harbor of uncorrupted will, and God will provide him with His aid."

Did her listeners feel insulted? Evidently not. In fact, Hildegard's sermon was so well received that the clerics of Cologne wrote to her afterwards to request a copy of it.

Hildegard's northernmost destination on this tour was the town of Werden, on the River Ruhr. She may have returned to Rupertsberg from there, perhaps traveling by land.

Even while she was busy with her second and third journeys, Hildegard worked on *The Book of the Rewards of Life*, finishing it in 1163. No sooner was it done, than she immediately started on a new project, *The Book of Divine Works*. That was to be an eventful year. A charter dated April 18, 1163, from the imperial court of Emperor Frederick I in Mainz, granted royal protection to Hildegard, Rupertsberg, and its properties. The legal status of Hildegard and her convent had been in question ever since she and her nuns had left Disibodenberg—was Rupertsberg independent of Disibodenberg, or under its control? Now there could be no disputes. Rupertsberg became an abbey under imperial protection.

Chapter Eleven:
A Second Convent

Over the years, Rupertsberg flourished. Hildegard seems to have been a good leader, fair and patient with people rather than harsh and autocratic, according to a biographer who spent some time at her convent:

"When there were rebels in the community she did not immediately reproach them sharply or cut them off. Instead she used to overlook, warn, put up with, and patiently bide the time, until through a revelation from God she received counsel as to what she should do about them."

This same writer described the daily life of the nuns at Rupertsberg:

"...they refrain from work on holidays, and sit in composed silence in the cloister applying themselves to holy reading and to learning the chant. On ordinary days they...apply themselves in well-fitted workshops to the writing of books, the weaving of robes or other manual crafts."

Rupertsberg had become well-known, yet with success came some disadvantages—it grew more crowded with each passing year. What should Hildegard do? Turn away girls who wanted to be nuns? Tell them to go somewhere else? It would be a lot of work to build and oversee a new abbey, perhaps too much work for a woman in her mid-sixties— but that is precisely what Hildegard did.

Across the Rhine River, in Rüdesheim, stood an abandoned double monastery. It had been founded only seventeen years earlier, but was already deserted. Hildegard arranged to purchase it from the church authorities in Mainz in 1165 and founded a second convent there, Eibingen. Unlike Rupertsberg, Eibingen included women from the middle class.

Two stories high and built in the shape of an open square, Eibingen had a large courtyard with walkways and garden plots. The convent church was incorporated into the square shape, and took up roughly half of one side. Over the centuries, all the buildings of Eibingen have been pulled down except for the convent church, which today— renovated, restored and rebuilt after a fire—is the parish church for the town of Rüdesheim.

Eibingen in the seventeenth century. The church is in the lower right corner.

Both convents continued to prosper and grow. Rupertsberg had room for fifty nuns, and Eibingen could house thirty. With up to eighty nuns in her charge, Hildegard lived at Rupertsberg, and crossed the Rhine River by boat twice a week to visit Eibingen.

Hildegard's sister Clementia became a nun in one of the convents. In fact, religious vocation seems to have played an important role in Hildegard's family. Her brother Hugo became a cantor in the Mainz cathedral, after attending the cathedral school there as a youth. Another brother, Roricus, became a priest in Tholey, about thirty miles from

Disibodenberg at the headwaters of the Nahe River. A nephew, Wezelin, became a priest at St. Andrew's church, which still stands today in Cologne.

Hildegard took a fourth, final tour, in 1170, to six monasteries in the region of Swabia, traveling by river and overland in a large loop through mostly forested country.

At Eberbach, Hildegard might have heard a legend concerning the monastery's origin, which involved Bernard of Clairvaux. Thirty years before she wrote to him for advice about her visions, Bernard of Clairvaux had come here, searching for somewhere to found a monastery. It was said that while Bernard was there, a boar had burst out of a thicket in the woods and rooted in the earth with its tusks. Bernard decided to build a monastery in that spot. The boar was also said to have rolled great stones into place for the foundation.

After Eberbach, she went to Maulbronn, whose name means "mules' watering place." Just twenty-two years before her visit, some monks had stopped to water their mules there, and decided the place was so nice that they founded a monastery. Today it is a United Nations World Heritage Site.

In the Black Forest, Hildegard visited Hirsau. Her southernmost stop on this journey was the double monastery of monks and nuns at Zwiefalten on the Danube.

At the monastery of Kirchheim, she preached another sermon, like the one at Cologne, about the corruption of church officials. It was so well-received that a priest at Kirchheim requested a copy. That letter and Hildegard's reply with her sermon are in the collection of her correspondence—as is the sermon she preached in Cologne.

On the left bank of the Rhine, the monastery Hördt, which she visited twice, may have been her last stop. Perhaps she used it as an in-between point for visits to places whose names have been lost over the centuries. From Hördt, she would have been able to travel downstream, home to Rupertsberg.

Eight years passed. *The Book of Divine Works* had been in the making for ten years, since 1163, and Hildegard and Volmar continued to work on it. Then sorrow touched her life again.

Chapter Twelve:
Battles with Ink and Parchment

Volmar died. For sixty years Hildegard had known him and worked with him, ever since her days in the anchoress' cell. He was probably her best friend. She felt alone, even described herself in a letter as an orphan, working all by herself on the writing she felt impelled to do.

Again, as with Richardis' death, Hildegard lost herself in her work. She finished writing *The Book of Divine Works* in 1174, the year after Volmar's death. As if to overcome her sadness, Hildegard wrote some of her most joyous, life-affirming passages:

"...all living creatures are, so to speak, sparks from the radiation of God's brilliance, and these sparks emerge from God like the rays of the sun. For there is no creature without some kind of radiance—whether it be greenness, seeds, buds, or another kind of beauty."

"God has created humanity in the divine image and likeness. God gave us the ability to be truly creative by doing good deeds, by praising our Creator, and by never forgetting God."

Others came to Hildegard to take over Volmar's duties. Within the year, her nephew Wezelin came from Cologne, and monks arrived from the abbey of St. Eucharius in Trier, where she had preached in public on her second journey. A year later, in 1175, the abbot of Disibodenberg sent the monk Gottfried, who began a biography of Hildegard.

Hildegard began to exchange letters with another monk, Guibert of Gembloux. Guibert was an enthusiastic correspondent and wanted to know about Hildegard's visions: Did she forget any words she spoke while she was having a vision? Did they come to her in Latin or German, and if German, did someone translate them into Latin for her? Was her knowledge of scripture from study, or inspiration alone?

Hildegard delayed answering him, so Guibert wrote another letter, expressing his disappointment and asking even more questions: Did her visions come to her when she was asleep, or awake? Did she allow her nuns to wear crowns on special feast days because of something she learned in a vision? What did her book's title, *Know The Ways*, really mean, and had she written other books?

In response to Guibert's exuberant curiosity, Hildegard finally replied, in a lengthy letter,

"I derive no assurance from any capacity in me. Instead, I stretch out my hands to God that I might be sustained by him, just as a feather lacking all force of its own strength flies upon the wind."

"Still, I have always seen this vision in my soul, even from my infancy...up to the present time, though I am now more than seventy years of age. Moreover, I do not see these things with my outward eyes or hear them with my outward ears or perceive them with the thoughts of my heart or through any contribution of the five senses, but only in my soul...."

Guibert visited Hildegard after this letter, for four days in the fall of 1175, and was fascinated to hear more about her visions. Before he returned to Gembloux, he shared Hildegard's letter with the monks at Villers, a monastery northwest of Rupertsberg. Hildegard soon received a letter from them, with even more questions about her visions and the scriptures—a list of thirty-five numbered items, some with more than one question. Each one could have been answered in a moderately long essay.

"How is the passage 'A spring rose out of the earth, watering all the surface of the earth' [Gen. 2.6] to be understood?"

"In what part of the earth are we to believe that paradise was situated?"

"Can bodily things be seen with spiritual eyes, and vice versa, can spiritual things be known through bodily sight?"

Hildegard took the time to answer fourteen of their questions.

When her secretary Gottfried died in 1176, Hildegard's brother Hugo came to work with her, and a priest from Mainz was assigned to be spiritual advisor to both her abbeys.

The inquisitive monk Guibert reappeared in Hildegard's life in 1177, when he visited Rupertsberg a second time. During his visit, both Hildegard's brother, Hugo, and the priest from Mainz became ill from a fever and died. Guibert took over their duties as secretary and prior. He was the most challenging secretary Hildegard ever worked with. He wrote down her words, but felt free to make editorial changes.

Still, despite his editing of her words, Guibert seems to have had a high regard for Hildegard. He describes her and his impressions of her convent in a letter to a friend:

"There is in this place a marvelous contest in the virtues to be seen, where the mother embraces her daughters with such affection, and the daughters submit themselves to their mother with such reverence that it is hard to decide whether the mother surpasses the daughters in this eagerness or the daughters their mother.

"Besides this there is another marvel to consider here: that though this monastery was founded but recently—a short space of time ago, that is twenty-seven years—not by any of the emperors or bishops or the powerful or rich of any region, but by a woman who was poor, a stranger, and sick; yet it has made such progress in its religious character and in its resources that it is skillfully laid out, not with grand but commodious and dignified buildings most suitable for a religious community, with running water distributed through all the workshops."

In 1178, a year after Guibert became Hildegard's secretary, her abbey became involved in a controversy. She and her nuns accepted a young man's body for burial in their cemetery. He was buried without objections, most of the town attended his funeral, and his own priest officiated at the ceremony. Then the troubles began.

Hildegard's superiors, the prelates of Mainz, heard and believed reports that the young man had been excommunicated. They ordered her to exhume the body and remove it from their cemetery.

Hildegard knew otherwise, but before she could convince them that she was right, the church authorities put restrictions on Rupertsberg. Among other things, the nuns were forbidden to sing the Divine Office, which was their spiritual discipline and the focus of their religious work. This was a real punishment to them all.

Hildegard wrote a letter to the prelates of Mainz to get the restrictions lifted, and delivered it in person, pleading with them. Singing, she argued, was necessary to the proper observance of the Divine Office.

"The body is the garment of the soul and it is the soul which gives life to the voice. That's why the body must raise its voice in harmony with the soul for the praise of God," she wrote. The prelates would not listen to her, so Hildegard sought help from another source.

This time, Philip, archbishop of Cologne, was her champion. Philip went to Mainz, taking with him the priest who had lifted the ban of excommunication from the young man, and a knight who had been absolved of excommunication at the same time as the young man, for the same misdeed, by the same priest. The knight had witnesses and proof to convince the Mainz church authorities. Eventually, the bans imposed on Hildegard's abbey were lifted in March of 1179, after months of dispute. The Divine Office was restored, complete with the singing of psalms, and music could be heard once again at Rupertsberg.

Just six months later, on September 17, 1179, Hildegard died and was buried at Rupertsberg. She was eighty-one years old when she finished her life's journey, a remarkable age in those days. Several times after her death, church officials took steps to canonize Hildegard as a saint, but for various reasons they did not complete the steps. Even so, she has been beatified, and Catholic churches in Germany celebrate September 17 each year as the feast day of Saint Hildegard.

Throughout her life, Hildegard refused to accept limits on her talents. She composed some of the most beautiful music of her time, yet we can discover no record of anyone teaching music composition to her. She preached, even though it was something most women didn't do in the Middle Ages. She wrote books that are still studied by scholars today, although she didn't have the privilege of a university or cathedral school education. Because she was so respected in her time, she was able to correspond with and influence the rulers of many countries.

Hildegard's writings and music are studied today by scholars from many fields, from music to medicine, theology to natural science, philosophy to literature. Nine hundred years after it was written, her music is performed, recorded and appreciated today. There is even an International Society of Hildegard von Bingen Studies, a group of over five hundred scholars in twenty-five countries who research her writings and life. As a writer, naturalist, composer, playwright, theologian, herbalist, and advocate, Hildegard left a legacy that inspires all of us to discover and use our own talents.

AFTERWORD
Hildegard's Homeland Today

We can still visit the places where Hildegard lived much of her life. With the help of local publications, it is possible to imagine what these places looked like in the twelfth century. A pamphlet describing local Hildegard sites in the Rhine region includes the parish church of Bermersheim, the town where she was born; Disibodenberg, where she was enclosed with Jutta; Rupertsberg, the first convent she founded; and the parish church of Rüdesheim, situated on the site of the Eibingen convent church.

Disibodenberg is a fascinating ruin and archaeological site on a wooded hill outside the town of Staudernheim. It is cared for and funded by the SCIVIAS Foundation, which promotes educational projects in connection with Disibodenberg, such as a museum on the site. There is a vineyard and wine business on the lower part of the property next to the museum, and a gift shop there has books and pamphlets about the history of the monastery. A meditation path ascends in a wide loop up the hill to the ruins. Signs with psalms and quotations from Hildegard's books and letters mark twelve stops along the way. The walk ends at a tiny, modern Hildegard chapel. Its rear wall of floor-to-ceiling windows offers a pleasant view of the vineyards and valley below. The ruins themselves are mostly low stone block walls, some with trees growing on top of them, showing the outlines of buildings. The ruins are silent, except for the rustle of wind through the trees.

Rupertsberg was ravaged during the Thirty Years' War, actually a series of wars which took place between 1618 and 1648. It existed as a scenic ruin until 1857, when it was dynamited and disassembled to make way for a railroad.

Part of the convent wall was used as a railway embankment. Today there are buildings and a small parking lot over the site, and only the ancient cellars remain. The cellars themselves are a kind of underground museum, cared for by a company that opens them to the public by appointment. The mortared stones of the cellar walls and arched ceilings overhead give a sense of what the rest of the convent might have looked like.

A short walk from the former site of Rupertsberg is a museum with models of what Disibodenberg and Rupertsberg probably looked like when they were active. It features exhibits on Hildegard's work and life, copies of documents, pediments (pieces of carved stone at the foot of columns) from both places, and an art exhibit of old prints and paintings of the ruins. Some of the old prints show people arriving by boat to picnic at the Rupertsberg ruins.

The parish church of Rüdesheim initially was the convent church of **Eibingen**. The church was devastated by a fire on the night of September 3, 1932 and has been rebuilt over the same site. It is in a residential neighborhood, and a post office is just around the corner. What a contrast to Hildegard's time, when letters were delivered individually by messenger!

Uphill about a mile from the former Eibingen site, the Benedictine Abbey of St. Hildegard stands. It was built in 1904 and has an active community of nuns today. Several Hildegard scholars have been nuns of this abbey, including Adelgundis Führkötter, who is listed as a translator of *The Life of the Holy Hildegard* in the bibliography.

In Rüdesheim on September 17 of each year, a celebration is held in honor of the feast day of St. Hildegard. The festivities start with the celebration of a Mass in the parish church, which has been specially decorated with flowers for the event. Some of the participants are clergy from countries as far away as South Africa. After the Mass, a procession of clergy, choir and pilgrims winds through the town, ending back at the church, a symbolic journey that is a fitting reminder of the life, work and travels of a remarkable woman.

Inspired by Hildegard

The seeds of ideas that Hildegard planted during her lifetime still flourish today. In 1998, on the nine hundredth anniversary of Hildegard's birth, dozens of performances, lectures, exhibits and classes took place worldwide. A bibliography published that year in Germany lists over three thousand books, articles, recordings and videos containing information about Hildegard, her works, her biographers, and their discoveries. That is a tremendous amount of material. While most Hildegard scholars end up collecting a lot of books, many people will probably encounter Hildegard's works without even trying to look for them. Hildegard's influence appears in many ways.

Students and their instructors read Hildegard. College students can find excerpts of her writings in their textbooks in music, history, women's studies, philosophy, religious studies, medieval studies, and literature. Translators continue to translate her works into other languages, so that they can be studied by more people.

Hildegard often got requests for copies of her sermons and music, and clergy often wrote her to ask for her interpretations of church writings. Because she was so important in her own time, her nuns made neat copies of her writings and correspondence and gathered them together. Hundreds of years later, from 1927 to 1933, the nuns of the current St. Hildegard Abbey in Rüdesheim meticulously copied *Know the Ways*, complete with its detailed color illuminations. Fortunately, the nuns had the foresight to create that copy, which they probably made so that they could study it without harm to the original. During World War II they sent the original manuscript to Dresden for safekeeping. It disappeared sometime after 1945.

Musicians and people of faith read Hildegard. Her words appear in prayer books, and her music appears in hymnals. Her music has been revived by the International Congress of Women in Music. Both professional and amateur groups study and perform Hildegard's music. Professional ensembles such as Sequentia, Anonymous 4, Gothic Voices, and others perform and record her songs. Amateur ensembles such as church, college and community choirs sing her music. Her *Ordo Virtutum*, or *Play of the Virtues*, has been performed many times in our own era in Europe and North America, using historically researched costumes and props.

Many contemporary composers have written music using the words of Hildegard's songs. Some of the composers write for unaccompanied singers, while others include instruments such as organ, bells, even marimba and percussion. Some composers use unusual combinations such as voice and electronic tape. Other composers use parts of her music, and add their own musical ideas to her compositions.

Composers and music theorists use mathematics and computer programs to analyze Hildegard's music. A mathematical model that composer Pozzi Escot developed for one of Hildegard's songs even appears as a series of polygons on the cover of a recording of Hildegard-based music titled *Vision*.

To hear live performances of Hildegard's music, try finding an Early Music Guild or Society near you. Their concerts feature music from the Middle Ages and Renaissance, for voices and instruments such as recorder and lute. If there is no group of this sort near you, consider starting your own. The Hildegard Publishing Company, cited in the bibliography, has transcriptions of Hildegard's music. With a choir director, singers, and sheet music, you're on your way!

Hildegard's writings on healing have an audience today. Readers can choose from at least fourteen cookbooks in

German based on Hildegard's writings and dozens of articles, papers, and books on her medicine. Doctors at a Hildegard health center in Germany use her remedies and dietary suggestions. Herbalists study Hildegard's *Natural Science* and *Causes and Cures* to see how herbs were used in the Middle Ages.

Over the centuries, many artists have created works inspired by Hildegard. Some artists paint handmade reproductions of the illuminations in Hildegard's writings, using traditional medieval materials such as parchment and gold leaf. A group of Canadian artisans in Quebec hand-carved Hildegard icons of oak and decorated them with gemstones and gold. Judy Chicago included Hildegard in her 1979 work of modern art, The Dinner Party, a symbolic banquet for remarkable women in history. The parish church at Rüdesheim has a Hildegard-inspired cornerstone and stained-glass windows, a statue of her and a giant mosaic of one of her illuminations.

Hildegard's life has inspired novelists to tell their own versions of her story. Playwrights have created dramatic works about her, and screenwriters have made videos about her life.

These are only a few examples of creative ways that people study Hildegard. You can find other examples simply by checking the shelves of bookstores and libraries for books by and about her.

What is it that makes people want to explore Hildegard's life and works in such creative ways? Perhaps it is the excitement of searching—a sense that there is still something new waiting to be discovered in her words. Hildegard scholars come from all over the globe and study many disciplines. I invite you to join them.

One of Hildegard's Remedies

"If a person eats nutmeg, it will open up his heart, make his judgment free from obstruction, and give him a good disposition. Take some nutmeg and an equal weight of cinnamon and a bit of cloves, and pulverize them. Then make small cakes with this and fine whole wheat flour and water. Eat them often. It will calm all bitterness of the heart and mind, open your heart and impaired senses, and make your mind cheerful."

From *Natural Science.*

As mentioned earlier, there are several cookbooks based upon Hildegard's *Natural Science* and *Causes and Cures.* It is possible to create recipes from some of her descriptions. The recipe on the next page is adapted from Hildegard's directions. It has honey, butter and salt, none of which were in her instructions, but would have been available in the Middle Ages.

Hildegard's Nutmeg Cookies

Ingredients:
2 cups fine whole wheat flour
2 teaspoons nutmeg
2 teaspoons cinnamon
1/4 teaspoon cloves
1/2 teaspoon salt
1/2 cup butter, margarine, or vegetable shortening
1/2 cup honey
2 or more tablespoons water

Preheat the oven to 375 degrees Fahrenheit. Measure the flour, nutmeg, cinnamon, cloves and salt into a medium-sized bowl, and mix them together with a fork until well blended. Add the margarine and blend in with your fingertips until the mixture is in small, oatmeal-sized flakes.

Stir in the honey and two tablespoons of water with a large spoon until it's too hard to do, then finish mixing with your hands. If the dough is dry, add small amounts of water a little bit at a time. You should have a dough that will show the marks of your hand and fingers in it when you squeeze it.

Shape the dough into one-inch balls and place them two inches apart on a greased cookie sheet. Flatten the dough balls with the palm of your hand to make cookies.

Bake for 8 to 12 minutes. Remove the cookie sheet from the oven. Scoop the cookies off the baking sheet while they are still warm, and put them on a plate to cool. Makes about 3 dozen cookies.

Select Bibliography

NOTE: Hildegard's writings are often known by their Latin names:
Scivias = Know the Ways;
De Operatione Dei = The Book of Divine Works;
Liber Vitae Meritorum = The Book of the Rewards of Life;
Physica = Natural Science;
*Symphonia armonie celestium revelationum = The Symphony of the
    Harmony of Celestial Revelations* [her music];
Ordo Virtutum = Play of the Virtues.

Baird, Joseph L., and Radd K. Ehrman, translators. *The Letters of
    Hildegard of Bingen.* Vols. I and II. New York and Oxford:
    Oxford University Press, 1994. Letters written and received by
    Hildegard. This is a work in progress. Volume by volume,
    Hildegard's correspondence will be translated into English.

Dronke, Peter. *Women Writers of the Middle Ages.* Cambridge:
    Cambridge University Press, 1984. Passages of Hildegard's
    writings, and commentary on them; has a 57-page chapter about
    Hildegard.

Flanagan, Sabina. *Hildegard of Bingen: A Visionary Life.* 2nd ed.
    New York: Routledge, 1998. Very thorough biography and
    discussion of Hildegard's works.

The monks Gottfried and Theoderic. *The Life of the Saintly
    Hildegard.* Translated by Hugh Feiss. Toronto: Peregrina
    Publishing, 1996. An English translation of the work of two
    twelfth-century biographers. Gottfried was Hildegard's secretary
    for about two years.

The monks Gottfried and Theoderic. *The Life of the Holy Hildegard.*
    Translated by Adelgundis Führkötter, O.S.B., and James
    McGrath; edited by Mary Palmquist and John Kulas, O.S.B.
    Collegeville, Minnesota: The Liturgical Press, 1995. Another
    translation of the work above.

Hildegard of Bingen. *Holistic Healing [Causes and Cures]*.
Translated by Manfred Pawlik; Patrick Madigan, S.J.; and John
Kulas, O.S.B.; edited by Mary Palmquist and John Kulas, O.S.B.
Collegeville, Minnesota: The Liturgical Press, 1994.

Hildegard of Bingen. *Hildegard of Bingen's Book of Divine Works
With Letters and Songs*. Edited by Matthew Fox, translated by
Robert Cunningham. Santa Fe: Bear & Company, 1987. At this
point, the longest English translation of much of *The Book of
Divine Works*. Includes forty-two of Hildegard's letters and
twelve of her songs.

Hildegard of Bingen. *Mystical Writings*. Edited and introduced by
Fiona Bowies and Oliver Davies, translated by Robert Carver.
New York: Crossroad, 1995. Selected passages of Hildegard's
works, songs, and letters.

Hildegard of Bingen. *Scivias*. Translated by Mother Columba Hart
and Jane Bishop, introduced by Barbara J. Newman, preface by
Caroline Walker Bynum. New York and Mahwah, New Jersey:
Paulist Press, 1990.

Hildegard of Bingen. *Book of the Rewards of Life*. Translated by
Bruce W. Hozeski. New York, Oxford: Oxford University Press,
1997. The only English translation of this work as a whole.

Hildegard of Bingen. *Hildegard von Bingen's Mystical Visions [Know
the Ways]*. Translated by Bruce Hozeski, introduced by Matthew
Fox. Santa Fe, New Mexico: Bear & Company, 1986.

Hildegard of Bingen. *Symphonia: A Critical Edition of the
Symphonia armonie celestium revelationum*. Introduction,
translations and commentary by Barbara Newman. Ithaca, New
York and London: Cornell University Press, 1988. Text only, no
music.

Hildegard of Bingen. *Symphonia armonie celestium revelationum.* Vol. I. Marianne Richert Pfau, editor and translator. Bryn Mawr, Pennsylvania: Hildegard Publishing Company, 1997. Transcriptions of Hildegard's music in modern notation are available in compiled volumes and in choral sheet music (octavo) editions from Hildegard Publishing Company, P.O. Box 332, Bryn Mawr, PA 19010, (610) 667-8634, www.hildegard.com; or the Theodore Presser Company, 588 North Gulph Road, King of Prussia, PA 19406, (610) 592-1222, www.presser.com.

Hildegard of Bingen. *Hildegard von Bingen's Physica.* Translated by Priscilla Throop. Rochester, Vermont: Healing Arts Press, 1998.

Maddocks, Fiona. *Hildegard of Bingen: The Woman of Her Age.* New York: Doubleday, 2001. A fascinating biography, thoroughly researched and very well-written. Includes an interview with a nun in the modern St. Hildegard Abbey in Rüdesheim, Germany.

Pernoud, Regine. *Hildegard of Bingen: Inspired Conscience of the Twelfth Century.* Translated by Paul Duggan. New York: Marlowe & Company, 1998. Interesting biography with many primary source quotes.

Silvas, Anna, commentary and translation. *Jutta & Hildegard: The Biographical Sources.* Turnhout: Brepols, 1998. Also available in an edition from Pennsylvania State University Press, 1999. Hard-to-access primary source documents that describe events and places in Hildegard's life.

Recordings of Hildegard's Music

These are only a few of the many recordings available.

Gothic Voices. *A Feather on the Breath of God: Sequences and Hymns by Abbess Hildegard of Bingen*. Hyperion CDA66039.

Sequentia. *Canticles of Ecstasy*. Deutsche Harmonia Mundi. 05472-77320-2.

Sequentia. *Symphoniae*. Deutsche Harmonia Mundi Editio Classica 77020-2-RG.

Sequentia. *Voice of the Blood*. Deutsche Harmonia Mundi 05472-77346-2.

Sinfonye. *Symphony of the harmony of celestial revelations: The Complete Hildegard von Bingen vol. 1*. Celestial Harmonies 13127-2.

Sinfonye. *Aurora: The Complete Hildegard von Bingen vol. 2*. Celestial Harmonies 13128-2.

Vox Animae. *The Soul's Journey*: Ordo Virtutum [Play of the Virtues]. Etcetera. KTC 1203.

Index

Text Acknowledgements

The publisher gratefully acknowledges the following:

The quotes on the pages listed below are translated by Anna Silvas, from her book, *Jutta and Hildegard: The Biographical Sources*: the epigraph, and pages 1-2, 3, 4, 37, 42, and 43 (Guibert's description of Hildegard's convent). Copyright © 1998 Brepols Publishers, Turnhout, Belgium. All rights reserved. Used by permission.

The quote on page 1 was translated by Carol Reed-Jones from *Acta Inquisitionis de virtutibus et miraculis S. Hildegardis* [the documents of canonization], edited by Peter Bruder, from *Analecta Bollandiana*, vol. 2, 1883.

The vision quote on page 11 was translated by Carol Reed-Jones from *Wisse die Wege*, the German translation of *Know the Ways* by Hildegard of Bingen. German translation by Maura Böckeler. Copyright © 1954 Otto Müller Verlag, Salzburg. Used by permission.

The quotes on the following pages are from *Hildegard von Bingen's Book of Divine Works With Letters and Songs*, edited by Matthew Fox: pages 11-12, Hildegard's letter to Bernard of Clairvaux, and page 44, Hildegard's letter to the prelates of Mainz, both translated by Ronald Miller; and the excerpts on page 41, from *The Book of Divine Works*, translated by Robert Cunningham. Copyright © 1987 Bear & Company, Rochester, Vermont. All rights reserved. Used by permission.

The quotes on pages 12, 15, 22-23, 24, 29, 35, and 36 are from THE LETTERS OF HILDEGARD OF BINGEN, VOL. I, edited by Joseph L. Baird & Radd K. Ehrman, translated by Joseph L. Baird, & Radd K. Ehrman, copyright © 1994 by Oxford University Press, Inc. Used by permission of Oxford University Press, Inc.

The quotes on pages 13 and 28 are from *Hildegard von Bingen's Mystical Visions*, translated by Bruce Hozeski. Copyright © 1986 Bear & Company, Rochester, Vermont. All rights reserved. Used by permission.

Illustration Acknowledgements

The publisher gratefully acknowledges the following:

The cover image is from *Welt und Mensch*, the German translation of *The Book of Divine Works* by Hildegard of Bingen. Copyright © 1965 Otto Müller Verlag, Salzburg. Used by permission.

The map on page xvii was adapted by Ellen Clark from a map in *Hildegard of Bingen, 1098-1179: A Visionary Life*, by Sabina Flanagan, 2nd edition, 1998, Routledge. Copyright © 1998 Sabina Flanagan. Used with permission.

The feather image at the top of the epigraph is from *Wisse die Wege*, the German translation of *Know the Ways* by Hildegard of Bingen. Copyright © 1954 Otto Müller Verlag, Salzburg. Used by permission.

The manuscript facsimile with the song *Laus Trinitati* on page 19 is from Dendermonde St. Pieters & Paulusabdij Ms. Cod. 9 (the Dendermonde Codex), by Hildegard of Bingen, introduction by Peter Van Poucke, copyright © 1991 Alamire Music Publishers. All rights reserved. Used by permission.

The illustrations of Disibodenberg on page 9, Rupertsberg on page 27, and Eibingen on page 38 are from *Hildegard of Bingen* by Fiona Maddocks, copyright © 2001 by Fiona Maddocks. Used by permission of Doubleday, a division of Random House, Inc.

The examples of Hildegard's invented alphabet on page 21 are from *Analecta Sanctae Hildegardis*, edited by J. B. Pitra, *Analecta Sacra*, vol. 8, Monte Cassio, 1882.

The photograph of Disibodenberg ruins on page 5 is by Carol Reed-Jones. Copyright © 2002 Carol Reed-Jones.

Printed in the United States
21721LVS00006B/190-228

9 780965 083317